Above all, prior vocabulary knowledge is important for these types of activities. Reading a variety of books and genres on a sustained, regular basis is absolutely essential for pupils to have success on grammar tests.

How to Teach Children to Complete Jumbl

Step 1 : Read the words quickly by scanning.
Step 2 : Identify who or what the subject of the sentence is (who/what is ...
Step 3 : Find the verb (doing word) of the sentence to find out what the sul......y done.
Step 4 : Choose the word/words that will form the sentence opener. These c......
Step 5 : Additional words, such as adjectives(describing words), can be added in if they make grammatical sense.
Step 6 : Identify which word is not needed in order to form a correct sentence.
  Tip - Write the sentence out if the child needs to visualise the words in the correct order.

Example 1 – Sentences beginning with 'the" :
  train   arrived   the   time   track   on

  The subject is   : train
  The verb is   : arrived
  The sentence opener is   : the
  The sentence is   : The train arrived on time.
  The superfluous word is : track

Example 2 – When a pronoun is the sentence opener :
  went   waited   he   early   home

  The subject is   : he
  The verb is   : went (Waited is also a verb, but it does not fit into the sentence.)
  The sentence opener is   : he
  The sentence is   : He went home early.
  The superfluous word is : waited

Example 3 – Sentences beginning with a proper noun :
  new   at   the   Sara   library   works   car   Birmingham   in

  The subject is   : Sara
  The verb is   : works
  The sentence opener is   : Sara
  The sentence is   : Sara works at the new library in Birmingham.
  The superfluous word is : car

Example 4 – Sentences beginning with adverbials :
  had   café   eating   a   yesterday   lunch   we   at   lovely

  The subject is   : we
  The verb is   : had
  The sentence opener is   : yesterday
  The sentence is   : Yesterday we had lunch at a lovely café.
  The superfluous word is : eating

Another tip is that, very often, two words that are similar are placed in the group of words and one of those words is not needed. For example:

pretty   she   nose   smelled   the   flowers

'Smelled' and **'nose'** have a link but **'nose'** is the unnecessary word.
The sentence is : She smelled the pretty flowers.

> Sometimes the word order of a sentence can vary. This means sometimes the sentence formed by the pupils can be phrased more than one way. These are often adverbial words or phrases. For example:
> On Sunday, we went to see the film. / We went to see the film on Sunday.
> Yesterday, the sun came out while we were playing. / While we were playing yesterday, the sun came out.
> I was eating breakfast when the phone rang. / When the phone rang, I was eating breakfast. / The phone rang when I was eating breakfast.

How to use this resource:

The main focus of the activities is that pupils can identify the unnecessary, or superfluous, word from each group of words. Words that are unknown or unfamiliar should be looked up so that children can learn their meanings and be able to use the words in other contexts.

The exercises in this book have been designed to gradually teach children how to rearrange jumbled words to make a sentence that makes sense and is grammatically correct. The activities increase in difficulty from the beginning of the book to the end, therefore it is recommended that children start at the beginning and complete the exercises in order.

Exercises 1 and 2 – Getting Started: These activities require children to practice rearranging the words to make a sentence that makes sense. Children should write the sentence on the line, using the correct punctuation and spellings.

Exercises 3 and 4 – Working Towards Expected Level: There are 7 words jumbled up and one of the words is not needed in the sentence. Children need to select the unnecessary word and shade the correct box to eliminate the word, and make a sentence with the remaining 6 words. Children are encouraged to write the sentence underneath each question, to help them correctly order the words.

Exercises 5 and 6 – Expected 11+ Standard: Typically, recent 11+ CEM exam features jumbled sentences activities containing 8 words, one of which children must eliminate and then form a sentence with the words that are left over. Children are encouraged to write the sentence underneath each question to help them order the words correctly. Please note – in an 11+ exam, children are not required to write the sentences out, however it should be encouraged when they practice reordering jumbled sentences.

Exercises 7 and 8 – Extension (Timed Exercises): These exercises are designed to extend children's skills so that they can choose the unnecessary word from a group of 9 words, and to do so within a time limit. The recommended time limit is 10 minutes. With these exercises, children do not need to write the sentences out while they are choosing the word to eliminate under timed conditions, but it is good practice to go back and write the sentences out afterwards, so that they can be sure they have chosen the correct superfluous word.

Exercises 9 and 10 – Challenge (Timed Exercises): There are 10 words in each question, 9 of which are necessary to form the sentence and 1 that should be eliminated. More words in a sentence means the sentence types may vary, and children are encouraged to complete these exercises in timed conditions, typically 10 minutes per activity. With these exercises, as well, children do not need to write the sentences out while they are choosing the word to eliminate under timed conditions, but it is good practice to go back and write the sentences out afterwards, so that they can be sure they have chosen the correct superfluous word.

Exercises 11 and 12 – Multiple Choice Timed Exercises: In these exercises, children are presented with a mixture of groups of 7, 8, or 9 words and then given a selection of 5 of the words, from which they need to choose the word that is not needed. They do this by circling the letter accompanying the word, from A to E.

©2020 S4E Tuition, Leaping Learners Series. All rights reserved. No part of this book may be reproduced or transmitted in any form or by any means without written permission of the author.

The following sentences are jumbled up. Work out what the correct word order should be and rewrite the sentence on the lines below. Remember to use correct grammar and punctuation!

Example:

curled   bed   the   its   dog   on   up

The Answer is: **The dog curled up on its bed.**

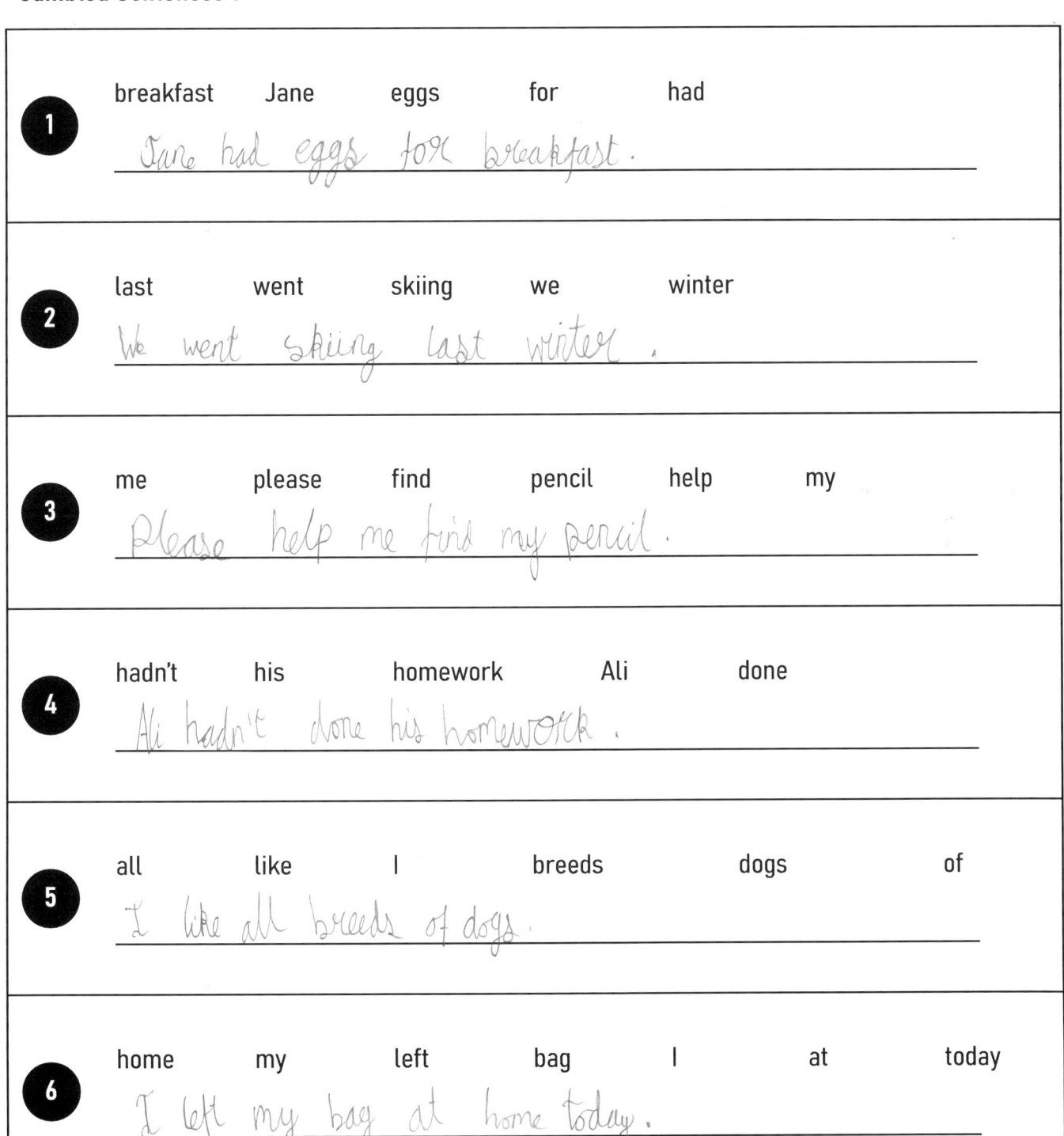

Jumbled Sentences 1

1. breakfast   Jane   eggs   for   had

Jane had eggs for breakfast.

2. last   went   skiing   we   winter

We went skiing last winter.

3. me   please   find   pencil   help   my

Please help me find my pencil.

4. hadn't   his   homework   Ali   done

Ali hadn't done his homework.

5. all   like   I   breeds   dogs   of

I like all breeds of dogs.

6. home   my   left   bag   I   at   today

I left my bag at home today.

7. wants　he　his　soup　lunch　for
He wants soup for his lunch.

8. too　go　water　the　was　cold　in　to
The water was to cold to go in.

9. beautiful　Alice　the　cake　made　most　had
Alice had made the most beautiful cake.

10. saved　sister　some　Lewis　his　for　cake
Lewis saved some cake for his sister.

11. bought　she　birthday　sister　gift　her　a
She bough her sister a birthday gift

12. pilot　would　be　to　Amy　like　a
Amy would like to be a pilot

KEEP GOING !!!

The following sentences are jumbled up. Work out what the correct word order should be and rewrite the sentence on the lines below. Remember to use correct grammar and punctuation!

Example:

curled   bed   the   it   dog   on   up

The Answer is: **The dog curled up on its bed.**

Jumbled Sentences 2

1. have   they   Australia   to   gone

They have gone to Australia.

2. enjoy   eating   birds   seeds

Birds enjoy eating seeds

3. called   hamster   Zara's   Charlie   was

Zara's hamster is called Charlie

4. preferred   Sami's   rugby   sport   is

Sami's preferred sport is rugby.

5. completely   cinema   was   the   full

The cinema was completely full

6. school   at   nine   I   to   walked

I walked to school at nine

7 comedian us stories the funny told
The comedian told us funny stories

8 are too going you concert to the
You want to go to the concert too?

9 dessert them shared he with his

10 must for revise I today exams
I must revise for the exam today

11 to going enjoy they all ballet the

12 noise the becoming loud was very

Well done! You have practised putting the mixed up words into the correct order so that the sentences make sense. Now, it's time to practise ordering words to make a correct sentence, while at the same time selecting one word that is the unnecessary (also called 'superfluous') word within the group! Have a look at the next activity...

The following sentences are jumbled up. Each sentence contains one word that does not belong. Work out the sentence and shade the unnecessary (superfluous) word. 03/03-23

Example:

sleepy   took   **slept**   puppy   the   nap   a

The sentence is: <u>The sleepy puppy took a nap.</u>

Jumbled Sentences 3

1. will   to   as   tomorrow   I   China   fly

2. a   apple   balanced   you   diet   strong   keeps

3. favourite   colour   Ronald's   blue   paint   is   light

4. mice   the   has   the   have   infested   warehouse

5. Roger   with   always   me   of   is   fighting

6. pass   will   tarts   the   me   please   jam

7 extremely braces make stiff shoes jaw my

8 monarch crown our Charles next is Prince

9 do litter green not the park please

10 sport ice favourite hockey player is my

11 other prettiest garden our flowers the has

12 all he has homework his play finished

13. gave he today a Betty jewel their

14. like French speaks Frenchman word Harry a

15. my I laundry and with mother help

16. Nancy today thirteen less is years old

17. carefully very to must listen the teacher

18. sky of is full has the clouds

19. is friend from Aziz at my India

20. in today served sandwiches have been ham

21. socks me for is Granny knitting or

22. the is eyes for in good fish

23. brightly glow is sun shining today the

24. test because English the taking is everyone

The following sentences are jumbled up. Each sentence contains one word that does not belong. Work out the sentence and shade the unnecessary (superfluous) word.

Example:

sleepy   took   slept   puppy   the   nap   a

The sentence is: **The sleepy puppy took a nap.**

Jumbled Sentences 4

1. relieve   liquids   warm   a   help   cold   dry

2. is   teacher   boarding   to   school   going   she

3. lovely   loudly   is   bad   a   chewing   habit

4. I   gets   well   ever   soon   he   hope

5. father   his   look   alike   Andrew   and   like

6. her   by   is   everyone   generosity   admired   from

7 is here water a castle there around

8 with all passed flying us colours we

9 England President the visiting is do American

10 as oranges as apples taste is good

11 has started colder have get it to

12 into swimming Michael an pool jumped the

13 shall please you door the shut behind

14 my drink mother they to loves tea

15 son little playing before outdoors enjoys their

16 were sold Christmas everywhere cards where being

17 we the going with are to cinema

18 us Julian look must after wait help

19 an   are   is   cook   mother   my   excellent

20 getting   were   the   impatient   quite   passengers   lot

21 the   the   teacher   angrily   shushed   children   or

22 now   going   am   bed   for   to   I

23 are   very   troublesome   a   is   throat   sore

24 had   a   shelves   the   dust   on   settled

The following sentences are jumbled up. Each sentence contains one word that does not belong. Work out the sentence and shade the unnecessary (superfluous) word.

Example:

curled	bed	tail	the	its	dog	on	up
☐	☐	■	☐	☐	☐	☐	☐

The sentence is : <u>The dog curled up on its bed.</u>

Jumbled Sentences 5   03/03-16

1. flight · it · is · my · are · is · unfortunate · delayed

2. in · black · a · dress · looked · pretty · she · wonder

3. wedding · anniversary · is · cousin's · my · tomorrow · it · brother

4. instruments · very · musical · almost · kate · all · can · play

5. ceiling · there · left · on · spider · a · is · the

6. are · my · in · both · prefects · they · school · siblings

7 books   is   encouraged   my   home   vocabulary   in   reading

8 accidentally   my   stepped   on   paw   cat's   into   I

9 stare   to   at   impolite   is   it   look   people

10 to   the   him   anthem   sing   national   everyone   rose

11 lead   sings   in   an   the   Martin   the   choir

12 crossed   mind   an   brain   idea   excellent   her   suddenly

13. not | I | the | native | speaker | am | a | English

14. beautiful | manners | habit | he | his | for | is | praised

15. will | they | are | anyone | cheats | if | disqualified | be

16. purple | the | we | rainbow | outside | behold | gathered | to

17. to | my | come | party | invited | everyone | was | birthday

18. Peter | an | had | he | lost | the | jacket | found

19	like	some	from	toast	would	I	breakfast	for
20	he	able	answer	everything	him	was	correctly	to
21	her	we	teaching	is	father	to	drive	her
22	by	an	overcoat	is	too	hot	for	it
23	we	go	to	plan	Sunday	wave	surfing	on
24	of	head	democracy	state	monarch	is	the	the

KEEP GOING !!!

The following sentences are jumbled up. Each sentence contains one word that does not belong. Work out the sentence and shade the unnecessary (superfluous) word.

Example:

curled   bed   tail   the   its   dog   on   up

The sentence is: **The dog curled up on its bed.**

Jumbled Sentences 6

1. am   all   not   you   I   if   go   late

2. with   you   for   exams   your   well   study   must

3. all   honest   by   an   admired   is   their   man

4. very   they   will   grand   had   feast   prepared   a

5. me   hoot   I   an   heard   at   owl   midnight

6. at   beat   easily   tennis   he   table   me   for

7 can　Liz　well　dance　and　with　sing　equally

8 them　an　honoured　with　gold　principal　medals　the

9 we　pencil　in　fun　school　have　plenty　of

10 flowers　favourite　after　roses　my　are　orchids　best

11 the　he　above　watched　balloons　a　soar　him

12 a　must　with　to　exercise　healthy　remain　is

13. is Sam to with able quickly run very

14. by the fireplace hands hot our warmed we

15. very pets far I twelve have so had

16. when we for drove to miles there get

17. cards from my found been of deck has

18. watch we beautiful want loving to the sunset

19	talk	an	let	a	good	you	will	doctor
	☐	☐	☐	☐	☐	☐	☐	☐

20	to	us	invited	of	their	over	farmhouse	they
	☐	☐	☐	☐	☐	☐	☐	☐

21	speaks	she	softly	too	speak	be	heard	to
	☐	☐	☐	☐	☐	☐	☐	☐

22	book	holy	Christians'	Christ	is	the	the	Bible
	☐	☐	☐	☐	☐	☐	☐	☐

23	handsome	is	many	look	to	at	very	Daniel
	☐	☐	☐	☐	☐	☐	☐	☐

24	to	learn	difficult	it	was	skate	to	were
	☐	☐	☐	☐	☐	☐	☐	☐

Well done! You have been doing well at selecting the superfluous word to eliminate and work out what the sentence should say. Can you complete the next activities within a certain amount of time? Have a look at the next activity...

> You are getting much better at ordering the sentences and identifying the superfluous word! Now, try to complete the following activities in 10 minutes. Set a timer!

Example:

curled	bed	tail	the	its	dog	on	up	new
☐	☐	■	☐	☐	☐	☐	☐	☐

The sentence is : <u>The dog curled up on its new bed.</u>

Jumbled Sentences 7   03/03-15

1. the — detective — as — the — acted — local — police's — siren — assistant

2. either — you — win — or — me — will — I — competition — the

3. is — my — o'clock — watch — nearly — in — it — by — five

4. air — the — plant — you — trees — into — purify — around — to

5. the — in — they — to — woods — camp — will — so — go

6. grateful — we — for — be — have — want — everything — should — we

7 for an respect soldier him service his a as

8 awful prevented knee a an him injury from playing

9 Tamara's new made Australia fur by was coat in

10 to idea good a is ever breakfast skip never

11 a famous children's is in she India author novel

12 to intelligent chess you helps learn strategise playing to

13 were class students new here our there twelve in

14 take mother us the to we will cinema today

15 perfumes make the is best France a known to

16 learnt little ride to they horses saddle children as

17 five proficient languages fluently or can four she speak

18 of is extremely grandfather fond cars big love my

19. the   remember   sink   under   the   memory   drill   to   put

20. will   you   help   can   when   she   always   Nina   do

21. are   plenty   there   to   from   a   choose   of   options

22. to   sunlight   shut   back   the   in   curtains   draw   let

23. stopped   important   always   tasks   best   give   to   efforts   your

24. that   father   him   anything   his   wants   buys   he   he

Great! You have attempted to complete the activity in ten minutes! How did you do?

You are getting much better at ordering the sentences and identifying the superfluous word! Now, try to complete the following activities in 10 minutes. Set a timer!

Example:

curled	bed	tail	the	its	dog	on	up	new
☐	☐	■	☐	☐	☐	☐	☐	☐

The sentence is: The dog curled up on its new bed.

Jumbled Sentences 8

1. father temper has cold his short like a he

2. the by shrinking completely flowers withered have will tomorrow

3. party was fancy tea to were mother invited a

4. like bustling the is nothing was countryside oxen cities

5. host he was admired for hospitable being are a

6. more I she much no believe cannot is that

7. beach | sisters | run | the | resort | inside | three | at | the

8. when | my | clean | arrived | I | room | she | was | tidying

9. us | Stephen | to | did | of | had | great | help | been

10. woman | secretary | an | and | organised | intelligent | is | the | would

11. Mr. | fiftieth | on | dead | Burton | passed | birthday | away | his

12. there | on | life | anywhere | Earth | is | but | stars | no

13. be   you   me   I   grateful   if   for   would   helped

14. enter   will   care   take   knock   before   you   to   please

15. mine   Alex's   together   are   hiking   and   my   going   family

16. tales   a   fairy   part   are   everyone's   childhood   of   of

17. their   schooldays   our   from   fathers   each   a   other   know

18. you   can   would   the   computer   as   as   sparingly   use

19 sleepover | I | a | am | friend | for | a | at | friend's

20 make | out | the | best | cakes | them | they | there | together

21 rain | today | it | is | that | must | unlikely | it | will

22 the | attended | he | Cooper | ill | although | instead | was | ceremony

23 Sheffield | in | they | a | into | moved | at | house | new

24 to | I | remember | shy | he | be | a | boy | him

> You are getting much better at ordering the sentences and identifying the superfluous word! Now, try to complete the following activities in 10 minutes. Set a timer!

Example:

sleepy   took   **eat**   nap   the   puppy   two   a   for   hours

The sentence is : <u>The sleepy puppy took a nap for two hours.</u>

Jumbled Sentences 9

1. gown   you   room   your   downstairs   on   dressing   put   before   come

2. anywhere   sparrows   than   are   I   are   else   rarer   here   they

3. prettiest   upon   dress   have   the   had   I   on   she   seen

4. airs   put   will   us   if   on   you   we   offend   you

5. too   everything   agrees   with   has   to   he   she   say   almost

6. was   friends   charming   very   befriended   everyone   he   because   so   him

7. girl   with   the   in   air   the   her   eyes   nose   walked

8. cannot   I   with   one   to   when   pound   what   decide   buy

9. how   wait   difficult   baking   soon   really   I   discovered   cakes   is

10. are   take   the   on   expected   Wednesday   to   test   we   study

11. Helena   was   entire   the   pie   tempted   to   eat   tempting   apple

12. affair   not   country   birthdays   in   the   grand   are   a   his

13. a he looks he short like foul in is mood

14. Albany wedding to her is engineer daughter in an married

15. now will you the time sit whole and sulk of

16. to allowed are stay past bedtime we passed our not

17. every her bounced her with curls of head movement nodding

18. into the assembly morning auditorium everyone twilight filed the for

19 the by many chief guest was choir the praised highly

20 to they us utmost all help are their doing every

21 valued be above for deserves to health else good all

22 I when assigned the finished time have you work on

23 the yet again be top grades form of will I

24 the Tony praise considers lose is the best high reward

KEEP GOING !!!

You are getting much better at ordering the sentences and identifying the superfluous word! Now, try to complete the following activities in 10 minutes. Set a timer!

Example:

sleepy   took   **eat**   nap   the   puppy   two   a   for   hours

The sentence is: <u>The sleepy puppy took a nap for two hours.</u>

Jumbled Sentences 10

1. girl   she   headstrong   little   me   my   is   a   sister   like

2. teammates'   play   at   against   was   captain   the   furious   foul   his

3. are   that   it   is   will   everyone   expecting   rain   tonight

4. scary   a   crashed   when   table   the   with   I   awoke   startle

5. was   the   haunted   by   ghost   very   house   malevolent   afraid   a

6. be   tomorrow   when   continuously   to   is   likely   it   raining   until

7 to understood accent him his foreign made be difficult he

8 their on behind my look schooldays fondly parents both back

9 from he at the thought frightened is surgery of a

10 in classroom encouraging Serena to are answer always teachers class

11 my it the until fill brim and to bottle take

12 of spite a fever to went in with she work

13. an butterfly insect slept Danny's he crawled arm up as

14. swimming but worth learning life are important and skills cooking

15. the already clock an nine was past showed wall it

16. tickets sold all been film have for the watching new

17. the owns cottage top hill the Edward of valleys on

18. she grows wants up medicine when doctor she to study

19. he an received up his when a compliment lit face

20. nourish is with moisturiser skin important one's it to by

21. invention of is an brothers Wright the the fly aeroplane

22. antiseptic hurt was wound apply I the to advised to

23. complaining George travels day thousands of each kind kilometres without

24. day a at grand swim beach sunbathing the they had

> Now find the superfluous word and circle the answer from A – E. Choose only one word to take out. Look at the example below. Can you do this exercise in 10 minutes? Set a timer!

Example:

curled   bed   tail   the   it   dog   on   up

bed	the	dog	tail	on
A	B	C	D	E

The sentence is :

The dog curled up on its bed.

So the leftover word is :

bed	the	dog	tail	on
A	B	C	**(D)**	E

Jumbled Sentences 11

1. should shall light read never insufficient you in to

should	shall	you	never	to
A	B	C	D	E

2. 1980s was a she actor famous the in their

was	famous	she	the	their
A	B	C	D	E

3. father's was mine it my belong watch was before this

belong	was	watch	this	it
A	B	C	D	E

4. the of was he exhausted end sleep by day the

of	exhausted	sleep	he	day
A	B	C	D	E

5. dessert is there finished you no for left

is	no	dessert	you	finished
A	B	C	D	E

6. hurry being avoid late we to so must

so	to	must	being	we
A	B	C	D	E

7. are Sean's extremely portraits of paints you lifelike

paints	are	portraits	you	of
A	B	C	D	E

8. in maybe partake protest will everyone the

protest	maybe	in	will	the
A	B	C	D	E

9. today least must degrees thirty it in be at

least	it	in	be	must
A	B	C	D	E

10. have Spanish teach her Carl on weekends agreed to

teach	her	have	agreed	weekends
A	B	C	D	E

11. bag are him for too to heavy the was carry

to	are	the	too	heavy
A	B	C	D	E

12. clue hidden was to the find an determined she

hidden	to	an	she	an
A	B	C	D	E

13. her to appear at on rashes started cheeks

to	on	started	at	her
A	B	C	D	E

14. in the coffee too sugar there off much is

off	too	in	sugar	coffee
A	B	C	D	E

15. leisure chair to read books for she likes

read	books	chair	she	to
A	B	C	D	E

16. they multiplication week teach school along at will this

teach	school	at	will	along
A	B	C	D	E

17. down bride below the aisle walked the

down	below	aisle	the	bride
A	B	C	D	E

18. she worried he his would away secret give broken was

she	his	away	broken	was
A	B	C	D	E

19. use frighten about fretting it no is there

there	is	it	frighten	no
A	B	C	D	E

20 at   interviewer   smiled   him   the   kindly   under

smiled	him	under	kindly	at
A	B	C	D	E

21 thankful   one's   all   ones   blessings   for   one   must   be

ones	one	must	for	be
A	B	C	D	E

22 advice   unsolicited   offensive   is   to   some   away

away	is	some	advice	to
A	B	C	D	E

23 way   tell   we   will   on   her   our   are

way	her	our	will	are
A	B	C	D	E

24 blue   eyes   shining   were   sapphires   his   was   like

where	was	his	like	eyes
A	B	C	D	E

KEEP GOING !!!

Now find the superfluous word and circle the answer from A – E. Choose only one word to take out. Look at the example below. Can you do this exercise in 10 minutes? Set a timer!

Example:

curled   bed   tail   the   its   dog   on

bed	the	dog	tail	on
A	B	C	D	E

The sentence is :

The dog curled up on its bed.

So the leftover word is :

bed	the	dog	tail	on
A	B	C	(D)	E

Jumbled Sentences 12

1. question us answer of know this knows the to each

to	knows	know	answer	each
A	B	C	D	E

2. perfume her has smell a fruity main

her	main	a	smell	fruity
A	B	C	D	E

3. following her was determined dreams to she in

in	she	was	her	to
A	B	C	D	E

4. let under in the a snowman build backyard us

under	a	in	us	let
A	B	C	D	E

5. breathing their to have us exercises recommended been

to	us	been	their	exercises
A	B	C	D	E

6. of many a he died attack heart

a	many	died	he	heart
A	B	C	D	E

7. keep water drinking to yourself hydrated keep for

to	water	keep	for	drinking
A	B	C	D	E

8. has pet at neighborhood in everyone least one my out

has	pet	my	one	but
A	B	C	D	E

9. wildfire to forest a the started in

the	to	a	in	forest
A	B	C	D	E

10. schedule an medicine you the with soon doctor must appointment

an	with	medicine	must	schedule
A	B	C	D	E

11. health sick friends Sally toasted and her other's each

and	her	each	sick	health
A	B	C	D	E

12. nor knew neither I he what would had happened

neither	would	what	had	he
A	B	C	D	E

Answers

Reminder – Some answers may have more than one possible way of ordering the sentence, but this may not always be written in the answers section.

Jumbled Sentences 1

01. Jane had eggs for breakfast.
02. We went skiing last winter.
03. Please help me find my pencil.
04. Ali hadn't done his homework.
05. I like all breeds of dogs.
06. I left my bag at home today.
07. He wants soup for his lunch.
08. The water was too cold to go in.
09. Alice had made the most beautiful cake.
10. Lewis saved some cake for his sister.
11. She bought her sister a birthday gift.
12. Amy would like to be a pilot.

Jumbled Sentences 2

01. They have gone to Australia.
02. Birds enjoy eating seeds.
03. Zara's hamster was called Charlie.
04. Sami's preferred sport is rugby.
05. The cinema was completely full.
06. I walked to school at nine.
07. The comedian told us funny stories.
08. Are you going to the concert, too?
09. He shared his dessert with them.
10. I must revise for exams today. // Today I must revise for exams.
11. They all enjoy going to the ballet.
12. The noise was becoming very loud.

Jumbled Sentences 3

The superfluous word appears within brackets at the end of each sentence.

01. I will fly to China tomorrow (as).

02. A balanced diet keeps you strong (apple).

03. Light blue is Ronald's favourite colour (paint).

04. The mice have infested the warehouse (has).

05. Roger is always fighting with me (of).

06. Please pass me the jam tarts (will).

07. Braces make my jaw extremely stiff (shoes).

08. Prince Charles is our next monarch (crown).

09. Please do not litter the park (green).

10. Ice hockey is my favourite sport (player).

11. Our garden has the prettiest flowers (other).

12. He has finished all his homework (play).

13. He gave Betty a jewel today (their).

14. Harry speaks French like a Frenchman (word).

15. I help my mother with laundry (and).

16. Nancy is thirteen years old today (less).

17. Listen to the teacher very carefully (must).

18. The sky is full of clouds (has).

19. Aziz is my friend from India (at).

20. Ham sandwiches have been served today (in).

21. Granny is knitting socks for me (or).

22. Fish is good for the eyes (in).

23. The sun is shining brightly today (glow).

24. Everyone is taking the English test (because).

Jumbled Sentences 4

The superfluous word appears within brackets at the end of each sentence.

01. Warm liquids help relieve a cold (dry).
02. She is going to boarding school (teacher).
03. Chewing loudly is a bad habit (lovely).
04. I hope he gets well soon (ever).
05. Andrew and his father look alike (like).
06. Her generosity is admired by everyone (from).
07. There is a castle around here (water).
08. We all passed with flying colours (us).
09. The American President is visiting England (do).
10. Oranges taste as good as apples (is). / Apples taste as good as oranges (is).
11. It has started to get colder (have).
12. Michael jumped into the swimming pool (an).
13. Please shut the door behind you (shall).
14. My mother loves to drink tea (they).
15. Their little son enjoys playing outdoors (before).
16. Christmas cards were being sold everywhere (where).
17. We are going to the cinema (with).
18. Julian must help look after us (wait).
19. My mother is an excellent cook (are).
20. The passengers were getting quite impatient (lot).
21. The teacher shushed the children angrily (or).
22. I am going to bed now (for).
23. A sore throat is very troublesome (are).
24. Dust had settled on the shelves (a).

Jumbled Sentences 5

The superfluous word appears within brackets at the end of each sentence.

01. It is unfortunate my flight is delayed (are).
02. She looked pretty in a black dress (wonder).
03. It is my cousin's wedding anniversary tomorrow (brother).
04. Kate can play almost all musical instruments (very).
05. There is a spider on the ceiling (left).
06. Both my siblings are prefects in school (they).
07. Reading books is encouraged in my home (vocabulary).
08. I accidentally stepped on my cat's paw (into).
09. It is impolite to stare at people (look).
10. Everyone rose to sing the national anthem (him).
11. Martin sings the lead in the choir (an).
12. An excellent idea suddenly crossed her mind (brain).
13. I am not a native English speaker (the).
14. He is praised for his beautiful manners (habit).
15. If anyone cheats they will be disqualified (are).
16. We gathered outside to behold the rainbow (purple).
17. Everyone was invited to my birthday party (come).
18. Peter found the jacket he had lost (an).
19. I would like some toast for breakfast (from).
20. He was able to answer everything correctly (him).
21. Her father is teaching her to drive (we).
22. It is too hot for an overcoat (by).
23. On Sunday we plan to go surfing (wave)./ We plan to go surfing on Sunday (wave).
24. The monarch is the head of state (democracy).

Jumbled Sentences 6

A superfluous word appears within brackets at the end of each sentence.

01. If I am late you all go (not)./ You all go if I am late (not).
02. You must study well for your exams (with).
03. An honest man is admired by all (their).
04. They had prepared a very grand feast (will).
05. At midnight I heard an owl hoot (me)./ I heard an owl hoot at midnight (me).
06. He beat me at table tennis easily (for).
07. Liz can sing and dance equally well (with)./Liz can dance and sing equally well (with).
08. The principal honoured them with gold medals (an).
09. We have plenty of fun in school (pencil).
10. Orchids are my favourite flowers after roses (best)./Roses are my favourite flowers after orchids (best).
11. He watched the balloons soar above him (a).
12. Exercise is a must to remain healthy (with).
13. Sam is able to run very quickly (with).
14. We warmed our hands by the fireplace (hot).
15. I have had twelve pets so far (very).
16. We drove for miles to get there (when).
17. My deck of cards has been found (from).
18. We want to watch the beautiful sunset (loving).
19. A good doctor will let you talk (an).
20. They invited us over to their farmhouse (of).
21. She speaks too softly to be heard (speak).
22. The Bible is the Christians' holy book (Christ).
23. Daniel is very handsome to look at (many).
24. It was difficult to learn to skate (were).

Jumbled Sentences 7

The superfluous word appears within brackets at the end of each sentence.

01. The detective acted as the local police's assistant (siren).
02. Either you or I will win the competition (me).
03. It is nearly five o'clock by my watch (in).
04. Plant trees to purify the air around you (into).
05. They will go to camp in the woods (so).
06. We should be grateful for everything we have (want).
07. Respect him for his service as a soldier (an).
08. An awful knee injury prevented him from playing (a).
09. Tamara's new fur coat was made in Australia (by).
10. To skip breakfast is never a good idea (ever).
11. She is a famous children's author in India (novel).
12. Playing chess helps you to learn to strategise (intelligent).
13. There were twelve new students in our class (here).
14. Mother will take us to the cinema today (we).
15. France is known to make the best perfumes (a).
16. They learnt to ride horses as little children (saddle).
17. She can speak four or five languages fluently (proficient).
18. My grandfather is extremely fond of big cars (love).
19. Remember to put the drill under the sink (memory).
20. Nina will always help you when she can (do).
21. There are plenty of options to choose from (a).
22. Draw back the curtains to let sunlight in (shut).
23. Always give your best efforts to important tasks (there).
24. His father buys him anything that he wants (he).

Jumbled Sentences 8

The superfluous word appears within brackets at the end of each sentence.

01. He has a short temper like his father (cold).
02. The flowers will have completely withered by tomorrow (shrinking).
03. Mother was invited to a fancy tea party (were).
04. The countryside is nothing like the bustling cities (oxen).
05. He was admired for being a hospitable host (are).
06. I cannot believe that she is no more (much).
07. Three sisters run the resort at the beach (inside).
08. I was tidying my room when she arrived (clean).
09. Stephen had been of great help to us (did).
10. The secretary/woman is an organised and intelligent woman/secretary (would).
11. Mr. Burton passed away on his fiftieth birthday (dead).
12. There is no life anywhere but on Earth (stars).
13. I would be grateful if you helped me (for).
14. Please take care to knock before you enter (will).
15. Alex's family and mine are going hiking together (my).
16. Fairy tales are a part of everyone's childhood (elf).
17. Our fathers know each other from their schooldays (a).
18. Use the computer as sparingly as you can (would).
19. I am at a friend's for a sleepover (friend).
20. Together they make the best cakes out there (them).
21. It is unlikely that it will rain today (must).
22. Although Cooper was ill he attended the ceremony (instead).
23. They moved into a new house in Sheffield (at).
24. I remember him to be a shy boy (he).